GOD IS MY THERAPIST

Inspirational Quotes,
Sc.

By: Shalonda D. Carlisle, LCSW, M.S. Edu

We all go through things during this wonderful journey called life, from toxic relationships, heart break, workplace issues, sickness, loneliness, death, betrayal and whatever life decides to throw at us, but we have to make a decision not to let those moments stop our destiny from being fulfilled.

This book will show you forgiveness, love, dedication, determination, overcoming and learning to deal with obstacles. Also, how I overcame self-esteem issues, betrayal, panic attacks, sexual abuse, death, situational depression, and allowed God to guide me. This adventure will be told through a series of daily quotes, scriptures from the Bible, and my personal stories.

Preface

In life, people handle traumatic events or stressors differently. There are options for help out there, including, psychotherapy, spiritual guidance, herbal techniques, etc. It's our personal responsibility to find out what works for us. The biggest challenge to face is taking the initiative to find something that works. This may be a trial and error period because everything does not work for everybody. But you have to be willing to push forward, try new things, and conquer the obstacles that you may encounter. As previously mentioned, I believe that we all have the ability to improve most circumstances that causes us distress; we just have to be willing to fight for it.

Formation World Tour 2016 Nashville, Tennessee

I decided many months ago that I was going to attend the Beyoncé Concert in Nashville, Tennessee. I thought it would be a personal accomplishment to travel to a city I never been to by myself. I felt like a character in a movie who decided to go on adventure. See all of my close friends had prior obligations or family priorities, so I decided to take that 300-mile journey alone to a new city and state. It would be my personal adventure. Although I was scared at first, I persevered and enjoyed myself. On the way home which was a 6-hour drive, I had a revelation from God. He told me three things;

1. He wanted me to share my Gifts.

2. Give my Heart to the World.

3. The time is now.

So, I decided to go ahead and finish my book of inspirational quotes, personal stories and bible scriptures that help me to move forward. This book will be told through devotionals. I believe this would be a great opportunity to share my testimonials and my truth. I hope this will help someone drive out the darkness and create many rays of light.

Introduction

He wanted me to share my gifts

Throughout my life and early adulthood, I wondered what my special gift or talent was? My surrounding circle consisted of individuals who had the gift of making delicious delicacies from scratch, selling products, applying makeup, styling hair, lawn & garden projects, DIY, singing, decorating, painting, healing others, capturing special moments through photography and other areas. None of these I would receive. I continued to ponder as time went by and I saw that I had the ability to inspire. Whether it was through small gestures, cards, or thoughtful quotes, I was able to turn a situation into a blessing. In the middle of the night, it came to me, that my gift was to inspire and that's when I started sending daily text messages in the morning to a circle of individuals via cell phone. This led me to start a Devotional and Uplifting Quote page via Facebook. I also made a conscious effort on social media to make sure it was uplifting, humorous and positive.

Give my Gift to the World

This means the gift to inspire. I wanted to reach people on a national level. The sole reason I wanted to explore writing books was to reach a multitude of people. My prayer was for it to turn into other opportunities to help others that may be experiencing some of the things that I've encountered. We often like to keep everything a secret. I wanted to let them know they are not alone.

The Time is Now

There is so much going in the world that affects us all and the morale of the country is at stake. We have seen racial division, police brutality, judging to a whole another level with social media, cyberbullying, political office candidates with no integrity and poverty. I wanted to elaborate on the three things God told me and where they originated from before we go down this road together.

Day 1: Yellow is my Favorite Color

"Don't let your situations Determine your Destiny."

Shalonda Carlisle

One of my favorite colors is yellow. The reason I love that color is because it can bring so much light into the room. When I look into the sky and the sun is shining, it warms my soul. Everyone's journey is totally different, some better than others, but it's the path that God has designed for you to determine your destiny. The journey is sometimes long but it all has a purpose. Have you ever wondered why someone else's situation looks better than yours? We must change that mindset. We must stop wanting or envying someone else's life. We must fix what bothers us and move on. God is here to lead and guide you, but you must be able to listen for further instructions and obey. We sometimes decide to go down the easy path and not focus on his Word. Remember, God will never leave you or forsake you. He will always lead you down the right path. You just have to obey his instructions.

Proverbs 3:5

"Trust in the Lord with all your heart and lean not on your own understanding."

Psalm 112:4

"Light dawns in the darkness for the upright; he is gracious, merciful and righteous."

Day 2: Chef Boyardee

"Don't let the Devil cook in your kitchen. Everything will catch fire"

Shalonda D. Carlisle

I never enjoyed cooking. Maybe because I was never taught the joy you can bring to someone's soul through their stomach. The right recipe or dish can make someone whole again. As a child, my mom was my primary provider and she was the definition of a hard worker. My mom would work 12 to 14-hour shifts. She learned this work ethic from her father who work 6 days a week to provide for his family of six, so there would be limited opportunity for mother-daughter bonding through cooking lessons. As time went on, not learning the Do's and Don'ts of the kitchen became a distant memory; but the other life lessons she instilled in me will last a lifetime. God has given me the necessary tools that I need for my journey and for this I am truly grateful.

Psalm 32:8

"The LORD says, "I will guide you along the best pathway for your life. I will advise you and watch over you."

Psalm 73:24

"You guide me with Your counsel, and later receive me in glory."

Day 3: Snap Chat Filters

"You can change your situation with dedication and determination, don't blame anyone, do something about it."

Shalonda D. Carlisle

Sometimes the inside doesn't match the outside. We all have camouflaged our appearances in some form or fashion. This could be by clothing, makeup, or the emotions we present to the world. For a very long time I looked happy and full of life on the outside, but on the inside, I felt dead, worthless and like a failure. These emotions went on for a very long time… probably 8 years. I could not shake the emptiness. I could inspire others for greatness but could not return the favor to myself. I have felt all the emotions of sadness, despair, disappointment, anger, and tearful. Through those experiences, God never left my side and helped me through the darkness back into the light. Joy will cometh in the darkness. Every experience that we have is an opportunity. We must explore the reason for the lessons, so that we can receive the blessings. As time went by I had to figure out what was bothering me and do something about it because I could only use a filter for so long.

Isaiah 41:10-13

"So do not fear, for I am with you;
   do not be dismayed, for I am your God.
I will strengthen you and help you;
   I will uphold you with my righteous right hand."

Day 4: No Sacrifice No Victory

"Anything that you are fed up with or don't like you have the option to change the narrative."

Shalonda D. Carlisle

Sometimes because of fear we don't want to let go. We become stagnant. Due to the unknown, we stay in that particular situation, even if we know it causes us long term stress that affects our mental health. We can already have signs that the relationship is unhealthy, but because of fear, we stay. We can be going through hell, but we think "If I show this person I am loyal everything will change". As years go by the problems get worse, yet, we stay. I've seen individuals stay in abusive and toxic relationships because of fear. We make up invalid reasons that staying would better for all parties involved. We become complacent. I don't necessarily mean a relationship with a person it can be anything that is unhealthy. We are afraid that someone else will reap the benefits of the time we placed in that relationship or situation. God doesn't send people or things to hurts us. He doesn't want us to have to endure pain to learn a lesson. We must understand that the devil operates in that fashion.

Deuteronomy 31:6

"*Be strong and courageous. Do not be afraid or terrified because of them, for the Lord your God goes with you; he will never leave you nor forsake you.*"

2 Corinthians 6:14

"*Do not be yoked together with unbelievers. For what do righteousness and wickedness have in common? Or what fellowship can light have with darkness?*"

Day 5: Fairytale Mentality

"I think we are so afraid of the unknown we continue to dwell in unhappiness."

Shalonda D. Carlisle

I was in a very miserable relationship for years. I was so afraid of starting over and continued to believe that if I stuck it out, I would receive my happily ever after. That never became true or real. I was determined, due to all the time I had invested, even when God showed me numerous ways that this is not the blessing He had for His child. I continued to ignore God, which continuously led me down the road of anxiety, financial stress and despair. I later realized that God doesn't want you to endure sadness to reach your blessing, although He gives us free will. He never gave up on me. As a woman you think that if you're loyal and faithful, it will work out. But that relationship led me further into an unhappy place. It was not until I put all my faith in Him and let go that I started to see the light.

Exodus 14:14

"The Lord will fight for you; you need only to be still."

Psalms 147:3

"He heals the brokenhearted and binds up their wounds."

Day 6: I'm Singing in the Rain in my Gene Kelly voice

"The Sky won't fall just because it's raining and storming in your life."

Shalonda D. Carlisle

This is the time we need to be thankful for all that He has done. I've noticed often that we pray for help in times of need, but we need to be thankful in those times of hardship as well. I can remember asking God to help me with something and in another breath saying if you help me I won't ask for anything else. This request was one that I would always go back on my word. I would continue to make that same statement repeatedly. I finally realized that sometimes we go through things to make us stronger and have more clarity. I also found out that we intentionally create our rain storms and won't bring an umbrella. As a result, we become drenched with water and mud. In those times of rain, hurricanes, and thunderstorms, we must be thankful for all that He has done for us.

Psalm 55:22

"Cast your cares on the Lord. and He will sustain you; He will never let the righteous be shaken be shaken."

Day 7: Totem Pole/Celebrity Status Syndrome

"Just because you can make someone your priority doesn't mean that they are a part of your plan."

Shalonda D. Carlisle

We often put so much into a relationship whether it be platonic or intimate. We often feel like if we show that person that we love them, then they will return the favor. But as time goes on you realize that is not going to happen. You find yourself treating others like they treat you. You find yourself becoming cold and bitter. Relationships often show signs of demise, but we tend to overlook it with a glimpse of hope for the future. I have had friendships that I would go above and beyond for. In those instances, I saw that they would not do the same for me. We often think they will see the light and make drastic changes in their behavior. We must realize that those people are not part of the plan and we must move on from that season and those individuals. God will always let you know when someone's season is up in your life. Every time I was in a situation-ship, He would give me warning signs, but I didn't obey His instruction and that led to more issues. We must learn how to pray and obey.

Isaiah 43:18-19

"Forget the former things; do not dwell on the past."

Let us not become weary in doing good, for at the proper time we will reap a harvest if we do not give up."

Luke 11:28

"He replied, blessed rather are those who hear the word of God and obey it."

Day 8: Career of a Lifetime

"Whatever job that you have' give it 150 percent. If you don't like your job find one that will make you happy and content. Don't punish others, follow your destiny."

Shalonda D. Carlisle

At my present job I see many people lose focus of the mission. I don't believe it is intentional. We often lose hope over the years due to lack of accountability, low morale, and ineffective leadership in the agency. I have worked several jobs where there were many dilemmas and unfair treatment. I also remember that I am fortunate to have a job and that I can't control actions of others. I always remember that our focus is to do the best we can do under any circumstance. I think this is when we lose our way and when the system is broken beyond repair. We tend to treat the job like it has done us, but we must remember that even when it's unfair and unjust that we are still serving a purpose. I have to keep in mind that Jesus always gave a 150 percent regardless of what man did.

Timothy 4:7

"I have fought the good fight, I have finished the race, I have kept the faith."

James 1:12

"Blessed is the man who remains steadfast under trial, for when he has stood the test he will receive the crown of life, which God has promised to those who love him."

Day 9: Marvel Movies (Captain America, Avengers, X-Men)

"Sometimes fantasies are so much better than our realities."

Shalonda D. Carlisle

My professional occupation is a Licensed Clinical Social Worker. I have been a Social Worker for over 15 years. Throughout those years, I have seen so many challenges obstacles with individuals and families. As a teenager attending Wingfield High School and naïve about the world around me, I didn't know what I wanted to be. During those times, the only professions that I heard about for women were Teachers and Nurses. As I started my new journey at the University of Southern Mississippi in Hattiesburg, I majored in Pre-Nursing. I soon realized that decision would be short lived. I realized that I was scared of needles and couldn't bear to take blood from someone's arm. I had to rethink my master plan. As I looked at the majors that were presented in the course booklet, I had to reexamine my field of degree. I stumbled over an introductory course in Social Work and I fell in love with the profession. One of the first professors and Social Worker I encountered was Delories Diva Williams. She had a smile that would light up the room. After taking her class, I knew this profession would be long lasting. The field of Social Work is not for the weak, it takes a special person to deal with the challenges that we face every day. During the past 15 years, I encountered everything that you have witnessed on the nightly news and movies you may have seen on lifetime. Social Work is one of the hardest professions because sometimes we don't have the luxury of leaving it at the office. In school, they didn't really discuss burnout and coping mechanisms to deal with secondary trauma. We have to deal with an array of challenges such as: sexual assault on children; rape victims; telling parents that their loved one is no longer here; working with families dealing with new changes in their lives; children being taken from parents; children who cut themselves due to how they feel on the inside; young teens having intimate relationship with adults and the list goes on and on. This type of work has a very high increase for burnout. We are overworked due to caseloads being high and not having enough resources to help our clients. As a Social Worker, we have to come up with ways to deal with burnout. One of the productive ways I deal is to escape to a faraway land that I know doesn't exist. I love Marvel Comics. I love how the creators were able to moderate those stories to the big screen. One of my favorite characters is Captain America. He reminds me of a Social Worker with super powers. In those movies, good always win but in reality, that is not always the case, yet, we have to find some equilibrium. If you consume yourself with all the worries of the world, sometimes it's hard to come back from it. I realized that God led me down the path of happiness with my profession. He showed me what was possible during this time and what I could offer the world.

Matthew 11:28-30

"Come to Me, all who are weary and heavy-laden, and I will give you rest. "Take My yoke upon you and learn from Me, for I am gentle and humble in heart, and YOU WILL FIND REST FOR YOUR SOULS. "For My yoke is easy and My burden is light."

Galatians 6:9

"Let us not lose heart in doing good, for in due time we will reap if we do not grow weary."

Day 10: London Bridge is Falling Down

"You can't climb to the top of the mountain with sandals on, it's impossible, you have to be prepared for your assignment."

Shalonda D. Carlisle

Since my early 20's my weight has been a constant struggle in my eyes. The mirror displayed a horrible mirage due to the way the media portrayed what beauty standards were. The media didn't exhibit different shapes and colors as beautiful. When I was growing up, beautiful was considered light skin with long hair. As I got older I realized beauty comes in all forms, but I also knew I wasn't happy with my weight. I know that I want to lose weight and feel better about my appearance, but I found myself not being consistent with an eating regimen and exercise routine. I've learned through this experience that until I change my mindset regarding this situation and stick with the plan, I will always feel this way and struggle with my weight. We must change our mindset for anything we are not happy with and come up with a plan.

Philippians 3:15-18

"So let's keep focused on that goal, those of us who want everything God has for us. If any of you have something else in mind, something less than total commitment, God will clear your blurred vision - you'll see it yet!"

Philippian 4:13

"I can do all things through Christ which strengthened me."

Day 11: The Enabler

"The old saying goes you can't help everybody. We must let people walk their own journey and stop sabotaging what God is trying to show them. We unknowingly block the process."

Shalonda D. Carlisle

There are two definitions of an enabler a person or thing that makes something possible and a person who encourages or enables negative self-destructive behavior in another. Are you that family member that a particular person calls if they're in financial trouble or have done something wrong and you've bailed them out continuously? Well you are an enabler. I don't think we purposely enable. We just don't want that person to suffer. Yet if someone continues with repetitive behavior, then we must let them find their way. I found myself continuously bailing people out and I was not allowing God to help them on their journey. I noticed when I continued to enable, I found myself receiving negative energy from the universe. We must get out the way sometimes and let God guide them toward their path.

Thessalonians 3:10-15

"For even when we were with you, we would give you this command: If anyone is not willing to work, let him not eat. For we hear that some among you walk in idleness, not busy at work, but busybodies. Now such persons we command and encourage in the Lord Jesus Christ to do their work quietly and to earn their own living. As for you, brothers, do not grow weary in doing good. If anyone does not obey what we say in this letter, take note of that person, and have nothing to do with him, that he may be ashamed."

Galatians 6:5

"For each will have to bear his own load."

Day 12: Forgiveness

"Don't let the devil use you."

Shalonda D. Carlisle

Forgiveness is one of the hardest things for me to do. It is an action that is better said than done. It's also hard for us as humans to tell someone that's the best course of action, but when the tables are turned, it becomes an action that is very hard to implement. For many years I didn't have a close relationship with my father; it was non-existent. I was angry with him for a lot of bad choices that he made. One of the major reasons was how he treated my mom. They were married in 1993 and I fought it every step of the way. I didn't even smile in the photography shots that were taken to capture their special day. As a 12-year, old kid I called myself protesting, because I told my mom she could do better. Time went on and my assumptions became very accurate. After my son was born in 2004 my relationship with my dad improved... but I never really forgave him. I was angry because every action that he presented I was forced to leave while my mother smooth over the thunderstorms presently in the forecast. As time went by, I figured

I was not only angry at him, but with my mom as well due to her always putting him first. I came to the realization that I needed to forgive her and him. When my mom died, it put him in very immobile state because she did everything for him. That task was passed to me. At first I was resistant, but I realized that my actions were not pleasing to God and I needed to forgive him, move forward and help him in any way I needed, because that is what true forgiveness is all about.

Colossians 3:13

"Bear with each other and forgive one another if any of you has a grievance against someone. Forgive as the Lord forgave you."

Ephesians 4:31

"Get rid of all bitterness, rage and anger, brawling and slander, along with every form of malice."

"Be kind and compassionate to one another, forgiving each other, just as in Christ God forgave you."

Day 13: Relax, Relate and Release in my Whitley Gilbert voice

"Let Go and Breathe If you keep holding your breath you will die."

Shalonda D. Carlisle

I was molested by someone at the age of 7. It was someone close to a family member. I didn't react to it at that time, but I noticed that it affected some of the relationships I would have in the future. I didn't tell anyone about the incident until my early 20's. I felt shameful and that it was my fault. I was also embarrassed to tell, because it happened long ago. What good would it do to let someone know now? Why tell someone now? Well I learned that I respond to others differently because of this. I'm not trusting of others. I don't believe in my son sleeping over someone else's house. I don't believe in children watching children and I have become emotionally unattached in how I express myself to others. I found that its ok to be consciously aware, but I cannot let the past define me. I couldn't let stolen moments that were taken from me define my destiny. I had to find a way to move on and move forward. We all have to do this in our own way.

Philippians 4:6-7

"Don't worry about anything instead, pray about everything. Tell God what you need and thank him for all that he has done. Then you will experience God's peace which exceeds anything we can understand. His peace guards your heart and mind as you live in Jesus Christ."

Isaiah 43:18

"Forget the former things; do not dwell on the past. See, I am doing a new thing! Now it springs up; do you not perceive it? I am making a way in the wilderness and streams in the wasteland."

Day 14: Negative People

"Sometimes God separates you from people that are not a part of your assignment anymore."

Shalonda D. Carlisle

I truly believe that if you surround yourself with positive light, darkness won't get in. But if it does the light will overpower it because it shines so brightly. During my time on this earthly plane, I have had the opportunity to encounter many people. Our human nature naturally expects everyone we call a friend to be happy for us. This expectation aspires from a sense of hope and inspiration. We quickly find out that sometimes that friend piece doesn't fit in the puzzle and we try to force it. We will have many clues and things that happen, but we look over it. As I haven gotten older or move into another level in my life, I always have to reevaluate if the people in my life are assets or liabilities. I question whether they are increasing my quality of life. We must realize, if a person is not helping us grow, we have to move on. The longer they stay the longer your growth will stunt.

Corinthians 15:33

"Do not be deceived; "Bad company ruins Good Morals."

Proverbs 12:26

"One who is righteous is a guide to his neighbor, but the way of the wicked leads them astray."

Day 15: Reach out and Touch Somebody's Hand

"Your Hand won't fall off if you ask for help."

Shalonda D. Carlisle

When I was about 6 or 7, mother and I moved into some apartments in the Georgetown area of Jackson, Mississippi. My mom did not know how to drive at this time and she would have to depend on others. My mother was very proud and strong. I remember walking to the grocery store because my mom did not want to ask anyone to take her. My mom was very dependent and a hard worker. I learned my strong work ethic from her, but I also learned not to let anyone else in and not to depend on others. This can be a gift and curse. Sometimes it's okay to accept help. We must distinguish the difference between being prideful and headstrong. I had to realize that sometimes God sends people to help you in your time of need or just to show that there are many people who love you and care about your well-being.

Proverbs 11:2

*"When pride comes, then comes disgrace,
  but with humility comes wisdom."*

John 4:10

"Humble yourselves before the Lord, and he will lift you up."

Day 16: Panic Attacks Year 2009

"Stress can be deadly as a bullet. Get rid of it."

Shalonda D. Carlisle

I was in a very toxic relationship for about 8 years. It involved heartache, betrayal, cheating and depression. I thought that if I showed this person, how much I cared, then they would change and do better, but it only became worse. I started to have panic attacks. I would wake up in the middle of the night and could not breathe. I would run down the stairs in the middle of the night for air. I felt trapped and no way to escape the horror. The panic attacks continued and after further research I found out that they come from stress. I knew what the main stressor was. However, since I wasn't dealing with the issues, my stressors came out in another form; panic attacks. I realized if you don't deal with something it festers into something bigger such as overeating, depression, drinking, or negative coping mechanisms. Mine came in the form of panic attacks. I knew then that I had to deal with the problem head on. I knew a long time ago that the relationship should have been over, but I was not ready to let go. I was blocking the blessings God had in store for me.

John 14:27

"Peace I leave with you; my peace I give you. I do not give to you as the world; do not let your hearts be troubled and do not be afraid."

Proverbs 12:25

"Anxiety weighs down the heart, but a kind word cheers it up."

Day 17: Sorry you have reached the Voicemail of

"When the past calls, let it go straight to voicemail, it has nothing left to say."

Shalonda Carlisle

Have you ever received a phone call from your past? There was a particular reason that relationship ended, of course, but as humans we have hope that the particular person has changed. So, we let that person come back into our life and then those same instances resurface. We must let go and start anew. We must learn to leave people where we left them and pray that God shows them the way.

Philippians 3:13-14

" Brother and sisters, I do not consider myself yet to have taken hold of it. But one thing I do, forgetting those things which are behind and reaching forward to those things which are ahead. I press toward the goal for the prize of the upward call of God in Christ Jesus. "

Corinthians 5:17

"Therefore, if anyone is in Christ, he is a new creation. The old has passed away; behold, the new has come."

Day 18: I can see your true colors shining through

"There is nothing common about sense."

Anonymous

This quote is a very true statement. We assume that everybody has sense. I remember working in a school district and listening to staff have conversations about a child's unruly behavior and how he didn't have any home training. In the same moment, one of my colleagues pointed out that we assume everyone has been taught the same morals and values. We assume that everyone knows the basics, but those things must be taught. I remember when I was in school that if the child didn't receive the discipline and structure in the home environment, then they were taught it in school. That has taken a back burner due to all of the tasks that have been assigned to the teacher to get completed during the course of the day.

Proverbs 22:6

"Train up a child in the way he should go, and when he is old he will not depart from it."

Proverbs 20:11

"Youth reveal their true natures by their actions, whether they do what is pure and right or not."

Day 19: R-Kelly Everyday People

"Sometimes the Ugly Truth is the Best Medicine."

Shalonda Carlisle

We as a society have made it acceptable to mock others, judge their appearances and think its comical to make fun of others' misfortunes. Worry about your own life and be happy. In May 2017, a new scandal hit Jackson, Mississippi. The difference in this scandal was that I knew one of the parties involved. Throughout the whole day people were judging the situation and only knew a portion of the story. I saw memes that were made that were hurtful and not entirely true at the same time. Spectators were talking about appearances and making assumptions regarding a situation that wasn't any of our concern. I saw now as a community, we can ruin someone reputation on suspected allegations or hearsay. I stepped back and thought we as a society have become the judge and jury. On that day, I realized how one particular perception can change someone's life in a brief second. During that time, I was guilty of judging other's lives that I had no business taking part of, however, I did not realize until it hit close to home. I didn't know those people I was judging no more than the people who decided to judge this situation. I decided I would make a conscious effort not to participate, engage, or make fun of something because it serves no purpose. We only get upset if it's someone we know personally, but we should have compassion for all.

Psalm 112:4

" *Even in darkness light dawns for the upright,*
for those who are gracious and compassionate
and righteous."

James 4:11

"*Do not speak against one another, brethren He who speaks against a brother or judges his brother, speaks against the law and judges the law; but if you judge the law, you are not a doer of the law but a judge of it.*"

Day 20: Life I am here! Don't start without me!

"Be on Time for the Rest of your life."

Shalonda D. Carlisle

It's a beautiful day to start a new beginning in your life. We all have a choice to accept or tolerate the things that make us unhappy. When you're ready to begin a new journey that's when you will see the sunshine.

2 Corinthians 5:17

"Therefore, if anyone is in Christ, he is a new creation; old things have passed away; behold, all things have become new."

Philippians 3:13–14

"One thing I do: Forgetting what is behind and straining toward what is ahead, I press on toward the goal to win the prize for which God has called me heavenward in Christ Jesus."

Day 21: Whitney Houston the Greatest Love of All

"Children are a blessing from the Lord."

Shalonda D. Carlisle

The year was 2003, I had just started the Advance Standing Master Level Social Work Program at Jackson State University in June. The University had a one-year Social Work program from which I could receive my Master's. My birthday was four days later, and I was engaged. Everything was working out great. But trouble in the relationship was followed by stalking, betrayal and infidelity. My aunt passed in 2003 at the age of 40. My grandmother was strong at the funeral. This particular aunt was very close to my mom. They were a year apart. Six months later my grandmother went into the hospital and never came out. She was put on the ventilator for issues related to breathing but never came off. I believe to this day, she died of a broken heart. My aunt became addicted to a substance she couldn't resist. The family sent her to rehabilitation centers, but relapse became common. My aunt struggled with addiction for years. She had two children. One came to stay with my mom and the other traveled back in forth from his father and my other aunt. Prior to my aunt's death, in late November 2002, she came to the house for Thanksgiving. I can remember my cousin fixing her hair. I remember her telling everyone that she was going to try rehab again and she and my cousin should go to hair school together. This would be the last time I saw my aunt. This dream became a distant memory because she died of aneurysm in January 2003. We found out later after her death that she asked my grandmother if she could go stay with her to get away from the city and away from the temptation, but my grandmother declined the request. My grandfather told my aunt later that my grandmother would hallucinate and say things like, "Tammy stop smoking in the house". The happiest time in my life, I thought, became one of the worst times in my life. I was with someone who didn't appreciate my worth and failed to realize it. One of the closest individuals to me passed away. Upon graduating, I found out I was with child. I stayed and hoped it would go back to the way it used to be but that was just an idiotic fantasy. Remember during this story. I mentioned infidelity. There was a young woman involved, whom I thought they were just friends, but it was way more. After everything hit the fan, I remember this young lady coming to the apartment we shared with a gun in hand and her friends. I remember this young lady stalking and harassing me while threatening to hurt my child. It was a horrible experience, but I overcame. My son was born in 2004. I remember being at the hospital my mom was there, my best friend, Marisa and my son's father, who was inebriated. Everyone thought he was in the delivery room with me. He wasn't… I was alone undergoing an emergency C-section, with no one to tell me about my son's birth. Those were memories that I would never be able to call my own. Finally, enough was enough and I had to let that negative season go. I gained two wonderful things from that experience: my son and strength to let go of something that wasn't good to me or for me.

Psalm 127:3

"Behold, children are a heritage from the Lord, the fruit of the womb, a reward."

James 1:17

"Every good gift and every perfect gift is from above, coming down from the Father of lights with whom there is no variation or shadow due to change."

Day 22: Jay-Z The Blueprint

"The Truth Needs No Explanation."

Jay-Z

I remember looking at the television screen and seeing an interview on Jay Z. One of the reasons I was intrigued by the interview was his delivery. He stated during the interview that the truth needs no explanation and these words have stuck with me. You cannot argue with the truth and never hide from it. I think with some of the experiences that I've encountered, I hid the negative portion due to judgement. I was ok with everybody thinking I was alright. I was ok with being miserable on the inside as long as the outside was polished. After all the years of hiding bad things that were happening it came out in another way. It came out through panic attacks because I was keeping everything bottled up. The packaging was pretty, but every surface starts to peel and crack. The truth shall set you free, is a very real statement. I had to make a decision to be honest with myself and ask GOD to help me through the process. Not only did I become free, I was able to start living.

John 8:32

"And you will know the truth, and the truth will set you free."

John 16:13

"But when he, the Spirit of truth, comes, he will guide you into all the truth. He will not speak on his own; he will speak only what he hears, and he will tell you what is yet to come."

Day 23: Papa Pope Monologues

"You are destined for Greatness."

Unknown

If you know me personally, it is very evident that I'm a die-hard Scandal fan or Gladiator. Every Thursday night I would be glued to my television, waiting to see what Shonda Rhimes had up her sleeve for the next episode. After the episode, I would be on the phone with my friend, Kawaski, for another 2 hours deciphering the episode or trying to figure out the intriguing, heart racing antic that she was going to do next. I love all the characters on the show but one of my favorites was Papa Pope aka Rowan aka Eli Pope aka Command. He was Olivia Pope's father and over the highly trained assassin team called B613. He was often seen as the villain, but I knew there was more to his character than that met the eye. One of my favorite aliases was Oliva's father. He would give the best monologues or speeches to put Liv down the right path. In his own twisted way, he only wanted the best for his daughter and he was her biggest fan. He knew that she was destined for greatness, so he gave her necessary tools to be successful in this fictitious political world. His words and advice spoke to me every time he gave one of his phenomenal speeches. It made me realize that we are all destined for greatness. But what path will we go down to achieve that goal?

Luke 1:37

"For nothing will be impossible with God."

Psalms 71:21

"Thou shalt increase my greatness, and comfort me on every side."

Day 24: Say Cheese!!

"Smile Every Friday and the days that follows."

Shalonda Carlisle and Sam Kazery

It doesn't hurt to smile, because it confuses the enemy. Often, times when we are upset, we don't want to smile. We want the world to know we're angry, but does this solve the problem? We must be purpose driven. We must make sure our armor is on when we are fighting, and the first line of protection is your smile.

Luke 1:37

"For nothing will be impossible with God."

John 10:10

"The thief comes only to steal and kill and destroy; I have come that they may have life and have it to the fullest."

Day 25: What about your friends in my TLC voice

"Every Friend Is Not a Loyal Friend."

Shalonda D. Carlisle

Signs, Signs, Signs... We all see them. Everybody doesn't have the title of a friend. I found out during my journey, that we assume people know what a friend is supposed to be. We assume that everyone will be as loyal, as we are until we start finding warning signs that a person doesn't have good intentions. I remember a particular situation where I had a friend who was close to someone that I really wasn't fond of. I remember that she would come back and talk about that person to me. As time went by, I started thinking that if she is doing this to that person, then I'm quite confident the same is being done to me. We must separate ourselves from individuals who don't have the same morals and values we have. We must understand that sometimes these individuals don't have good intentions. They only want to be around us because it's beneficial to them.

Proverbs 17:17

"A friend loves at all times, and a brother is born for adversity."

Proverbs 27:17

"Iron sharpens iron, and one man sharpens another."

Day 26: Tick Tock

"Time Heals all Wounds and time reveal all things, don't keep checking your watch."

Shalonda D. Carlisle

Have you ever gone through something and that moment when you're going through it feels like the end? I remember going through a bad breakup and thinking I would never recover from it. I found out with time and prayers those wounds did heal but I had to be patient.

Isaiah 53:4

"Surely he has borne our griefs and carried our sorrows; yet we esteemed him stricken, smitten by God, and afflicted. But he was wounded for our transgressions; he was crushed for our iniquities; upon him was the chastisement that brought us peace, and with his stripes we are healed."

Day 27: The Power of the Tongue

"Don't let Corrupted Communication Change your Character."

Shalonda D. Carlisle

Sometimes we let what another person says about us change who we are. Especially if the person is someone we trust or admire. I remember one time, I had an acquaintance who always had something very negative to say about everything. If you say one positive, then she will combat with two negatives. She could never see joy. I found out that she learned those behaviors from her mother. Her mother would also say negative things about her appearance, personality and achievements. As she grew, she spewed up those same learned behaviors to others. It was not intentional but that was all that she knew. We must learn how to fight the good fight. We must learn that just because someone says something deadly with their tongue, doesn't mean we have let it define us.

Psalm 19:14

"May these words of my mouth and this meditation of my heart be pleasing in your sight, Lord, my Rock and my Redeemer."

Day 28: Narcissistic People

"Best Response is a Non-Reactive Response."

Shalonda D. Carlisle

Kindness and silence are the deadliest weapons you can give to a person who likes drama and chaos. I have an aunt that assisted with raising me and I only remember fond memories of her. She would make sure my hair was combed and showed me nothing but love. I grew up, I noticed that all her relationships were complicated. My mother didn't have a relationship with her due to her toxic and manipulative ways. After my mother's passing, my maternal side decided to plan a family trip. She created so much chaos and confusion with family members. I decided that it needed to be addressed. So, my tongue used words that should not have been verbalized. Not only did I do something that wasn't pleasing to God, but I realized with a Narcissist you can never win with words. No response was the best response. When the family decided not to respond but pray, it did better than the war of words.

Proverbs 14:29

*"Whoever is patient has great understanding,
    but one who is quick-tempered displays folly."*

Romans 12:17

*"Do not repay anyone evil for evil. Be careful to do
what is right in the eyes of everyone."*

Day 29: Live in the Present

"Don't dwell on what you have lost on yesterday, focus on what you have today. Your future is in the making. Seek Him in guidance. You will persevere."

Shalonda D. Carlisle

I found myself going and continuing to live in moments that have caused me pain or when I made a mistake. I saw myself not moving forward because it was easier to feel in a state of complacency; whether it was taking an intimate partner back who constantly cheated or being molested or using my credit cards on items that I could not afford to pay off. During my childhood, I always wondered why I didn't have healthy relationship with my paternal grandmother. She never tried to be a part of my life. I never received a phone call from most of my father's family. I felt very isolated from them. No well wishes during life events or being physically present for them. The only time I remember receiving a phone call from my grandmother was in 2018 when my mother passed. I used to become very angry because I knew that was not how it was supposed to be. I received a different reception from my maternal grandmother until the day she died. She was always there for me for every life event and by contacting me on the phone to see how I was doing. I started to realize you can't let individuals make you feel a certain way. I had to learn to live in the present and learn that if a person doesn't make an effort to be a part of my life, regardless if they are blood or not, I have to be ok with that and not let that stop me from moving forward. I had to take responsibility, accept it and make a conscious effort to move forward. Healing is the way. In order to heal, you have to ask God for the guidance and come up with a plan to change the things that caused distress in your life.

James 2:14-26

"For just as the body without the spirit is dead, so also faith without works is dead.

Day 30: November Rain

"Your ambitions and drive will get you far, but faith in God will get you there. Network with a positive circle and delete defeated energy."

Shalonda D. Carlisle

As I slept one Sunday night, I heard my garage door open. I really thought I was dreaming. I heard a soft voice whisper those words that, once uttered out her mouth would haunt me forever. My sister, Shondell, repeatedly called my name and then says, "Shalonda Mama gone". I immediately got up to make sure it was all a dream but to my dismay, it wasn't. Soon after I turned the light on to pinch myself, I heard another person open the door and it was my mom's sister. I knew then that it was my new reality. I didn't know that three hours prior, that my mother told my sister that she needed to go to the hospital. My sister stated, "Mama verbalized that she couldn't make it out of the house and that she was going to die". After she uttered those words, Mama's eyes rolled back, and she collapsed on the floor, in my adolescent home. If I didn't have good people praying for me then I would not have made it through that time. Life is so short, so we need to live it. Surround yourself with people who will uplift you and show you the same respect in return. I realized that when you are around negative energy, it creates a slow death to your soul.

Revelation 21:4

"God will wipe away every tear from their eyes; there shall be no more death, nor sorrow, nor crying. There shall be no more pain, for the former things have passed away."

Psalm 147:3

"He heals the brokenhearted and binds up their wounds."

Conclusion

I would like to take this opportunity to thank you all for taking this journey with me. The road has been eventful, but I'm truly thankful for the good, the bad and ugly. I think in life we become embarrassed with our stories and keep them a secret, but you can't heal what you don't reveal. During my journey, God never left my side. He guided me and made sure I was covered through his blood. Stay tuned for God is my Therapist 2. I only touch the surface with my stories in this book. I have so much more that I need to share with you.

Dedication

This book is dedicated to Betty Joyce Norwood, my mother, who passed away unexpectedly on March 26, 2018. Thank you for all that you instilled in me and for being the best Mom you could be. Until we meet again. I love you forever.

Made in the USA
Lexington, KY
30 December 2018